How to Make a Sky Garden

Story by Suzanne Barton

Illustrations by
Begoña Fernandez Corbalan

How to Build a Sky Garden

Text: Suzanne Barton
Publishers: Tania Mazzeo and Eliza Webb
Series consultant: Amanda Sutera
  Hands on Heads Consulting
Editor: Beth Browne
Project editor: Annabel Smith
Designer: Jess Kelly
Project designer: Danielle Maccarone
Illustrations: Begoña Fernandez Corbalan
Production controller: Renee Tome

NovaStar

Text © 2024 Cengage Learning Australia Pty Limited
Illustrations © 2024 Cengage Learning Australia Pty Limited

ISBN 978 0 17 033408 2

Cengage Learning Australia
Level 5, 80 Dorcas Street
Southbank VIC 3006 Australia
Phone: 1300 790 853
Email: aust.nelsonprimary@cengage.com

For learning solutions, visit **cengage.com.au**

Printed in China by 1010 Printing International Ltd
1 2 3 4 5 6 7 28 27 26 25 24

Nelson acknowledges the Traditional Owners and Custodians of the lands of all First Nations Peoples. We pay respect to Elders past and present, and extend that respect to all First Nations Peoples today.

Contents

NO PETS
NO DIRTY SHOES
NO PARTIES
Rosie Ritz, Owner

Chapter 1

Runaway Carrot

Dad and I were in our apartment when we heard the voice. "Carrot!" it said.

I looked up from my science experiment.

"I think my veggie juice is talking," Dad said.

As *if*, I thought.

"Caaaarrrot!"

The voice was coming from the hallway outside our apartment.

We opened the door and saw a girl.

No *way*. No other children lived at Tarragon Towers. School holidays were lonely.

"Hi," the girl said. "I'm Daisy. I just moved in next door. Could you please help me find my cat? She's called Carrot."

Dad gave me a nudge and went back to his veggie juice.

"Hi, I'm Ash," I said.

"Carrot is ginger with stripes. She came with us from the farm," Daisy said.

"Rosie Ritz owns this building, and she hates animals," I said. "She'll probably take Carrot away if she finds her first."

Daisy looked like she was about to cry.

Oops.

"Don't worry," I said. "I'll help you look."

We searched the whole building. On the top floor, we saw a flash of ginger racing up the stairs to the roof. Daisy ran ahead, but my stomach flipped. Being up *that* high makes me puke.

TO THE ↑
ROOF ↑

Chapter 2

My Worst Nightmare

I stood at the bottom of the stairs. Bad memories flooded back. Like the time I got stuck high up on a broken Ferris wheel. And when I froze at the top of a lighthouse.

Not *again*.

But then I heard Daisy shriek. I forced myself up the stairs. On the roof, Carrot had pounced on Daisy. They were safe ... but my breakfast wasn't.

Ant-like people on the streets below swirled before my eyes. Then it happened, like it always does. *Bleurghhh!*

Carrot looked at me as if she was horrified.

"Sorry," I mumbled to Daisy. "Heights make me sick."

I waited for Daisy to run away in disgust, but she snort-laughed instead.

"It's okay," she said. "Just don't look down."

Easier said than done, I thought.

"So you moved from a farm?" I asked.

"Yes. The city is so grey. I miss trees and wildlife," Daisy said.

"There are *some* trees in the city," I said, pointing at some distant treetops. "Like, at the botanic gardens."

"We'd have to take the train," Daisy sighed. "Carrot wouldn't like that."

Carrot meowed as if in agreement.

"I wish we never had to move here for Mum's job ... but at least I've made a friend," Daisy said, smiling at me.

Friend? I thought, grinning. Then I babbled something *really* silly.

"My science book says some people grow trees on rooftops," I said. "It helps cool the city."

"A sky garden!" Daisy squealed. "Let's make one here!"

Me and my big mouth. A sky garden ... more like a vomit garden.

Before I could speak, Rosie Ritz stomped onto the roof.

"Trespassers!" she roared.

Chapter 3

Rage on the Roof

Rosie's cheeks were flushed with rage. Even her hair seemed angry. "What are you two doing up here?" she growled.

"We were talking about building a garden here on the roof," Daisy said.

"In your dreams," Rosie snapped. "I'm building a helipad."

Daisy's shoulders slumped.

"Celebrities will pay megabucks to live here," Rosie said. "They love helicopters."

"Celebrities also love trees and flowers," Daisy said.

Come on. Say something.

"B-b-bees love flowers," I stammered.

"Is that a cat?" Rosie interrupted. "Get it out of here – no pets are allowed!"

She turned to leave, then spun back around. "Construction of the helipad starts in one week. Stay out of my sight!"

"She's really mad," I said. "We should go home."

"We're just giving up?" Daisy asked. "No sky garden?"

I didn't know what to say.

"It's my birthday this weekend," Daisy said. "It'll be my first one in this boring, grey city. And my saddest one ever."

Daisy ran home in tears.

This must be the world's shortest friendship.

Chapter 4

Surprise Superheroes

The next morning, I heard Daisy playing sad, squeaky songs on her clarinet through the wall. I told Dad everything that had happened yesterday.

"Sounds like there's no stopping Rosie's helipad," Dad said. "But I'm sure you can find a way to cheer up your new friend."

I looked at my science experiment.

"Maybe I could make a *small* sky garden," I said. "Just for Daisy's birthday."

I worked hard in secret for days.
Dad helped me borrow a trolley, tools and some plants from the neighbours. Mrs Liu from upstairs even gave me a statue of a flamingo to decorate the garden.

Once I was on the roof, I never looked down. But even after all my work, the sky garden looked nothing like the pictures in my science book.

The next day was Daisy's birthday. She left in the morning for a day out with her mum, looking gloomy. All seemed lost, until a crew of breakdancing grannies arrived at my door.

"I posted about your garden on GrannyChat," Mrs Liu said. "My hip-hop dance club wants to help."

We all headed up to the roof, and word spread fast.

By lunchtime, lots of people were working side by side. Some builders working on the apartment block next door saw what we were doing and came to lend a hand. Dad's beekeeper friend even brought some hives.

This just might work.

Later that afternoon, there it was: our sky garden, ready for a party. When Daisy and her mum arrived home, I led them to the roof. Daisy stared in amazement.

"Wow, you did it! You made a sky garden!" she said. "This is the best birthday ever. Thank you, Ash."

As the party continued, more neighbours joined us. I didn't even think about being up high. Everything was perfect ... until Rosie Ritz burst through the door.

Chapter 5

The Famous Friends

"What do you call this?" Rosie hissed.

"It's a sky garden," I said. "We planted some roses just for you."

Rosie sniffed a bloom and calmed down ... for about two seconds.

"Everyone, go home!" she boomed. "Get off my helipad."

Suddenly, Mrs Liu whooped. "The sky garden is a sensation," she said. "I'm live-streaming the party and thousands of people are watching. Say hello, Rosie!"

Rosie waved at the phone awkwardly.

Mrs Liu winked at us as she pop-and-lock danced away.

Rosie looked around at the smiling crowd. "Fine. Keep your sky garden ... for now."

Just then, a tiny ball of fuzz headbutted Rosie's ankle. Rosie glared down. A kitten gazed up.

"Carrot had babies!" Daisy said.

Rosie scooped up the kitten.

Uh oh. Rosie's going to scream.

But then she actually smiled. She pulled the kitten close to her ear, listening to it purr.

Over the weeks and months that followed, the sky garden grew. Wildlife moved in. Neighbours became friends. And I didn't puke once.

Rosie even got her wish to hang out with celebrities – my friend Daisy and I were famous.

LOCAL KIDS SHOW THE NEIGHBOURHOOD HOW TO BUILD A SKY GARDEN